Native American Tales

Retold by Saviour Pirotta

Illustrated by Richard Hook and Claire Robinson

WAYLAND

Traditional Stories

African Tales
Native American Tales

Editor: Cath Senker
Cover design: Dennis Day

First published in 1998 by Wayland Publishers Ltd,
61 Western Road, Hove, East Sussex, BN3 1JD, England

British Library Cataloguing in Publication Data
Pirotta, Saviour
Native American Tales. – Simplified ed. – (Traditional Stories)
I. Tales – North America – Juvenile literature
I. Title II. Hook, Richard III. Robinson, Claire IV. Hull, Robert
Native North American Stories
398.2'097

ISBN 0 7502 2271 9

Typeset by Cath Senker
Printed and bound in Italy
by G. Canale & C. S.p.A. - Borgaro T.se (Turin)

This book is based on the original title *Native North American Stories*, published in 1992 by Wayland Publishers Ltd.
Colour artwork by Richard Hook
Line artwork by Claire Robinson. Map artwork on page 47 by Peter Bull.

Contents

Introduction

Some 30,000 years ago a strip of land connected Siberia to America. A group of people crossed this strip of land and settled in what is now Alaska. Their descendants slowly spread over the whole of the American continent, settling in both North and South America.

These first Americans were divided into many different peoples: the Blackfoot, Lakota, Iroquois, Pawnee, Pima, Tsimshian, Sioux, Cree, Navajo, Crow and hundreds of others.

They all had their own customs and their own language. Some lived in *tipis*; others preferred longhouses or wigwams. In the far north, the Inuit built ice houses with whale bones for rafters. In the summer they lived in tents made from seal or caribou skins.

For thousands of years their lives stayed relatively unchanged. When they were sick or in trouble they sought the help of their medicine man. They respected and obeyed their chief. Some hunted buffalo and fished. Others farmed the land. The women wove clothes and made arrows. In the evening, they sat around the fire and told stories.

They knew hundreds, perhaps thousands, of tales. Some were grand religious myths that explained how the world was made and filled with living creatures. Others were stories about how the Spirits gave the birds their colours, the animals their habits and the people their crops. Many were simple tales about animals, usually meant to teach children something about the world.

They had funny tales too, about rascals like Coyote and Hare. Some told stories about life and death, and about great heroes who brought honour to their people. And they had creepy ghost stories too, to chill the listeners' blood.

For thousands of years these stories were not written down. They were kept alive by the storytellers, who told them to children and adults over and over again. Now many of these stories have been written in books, so that people all over the world can read and enjoy them.

Here are just a few of them.

Raven

The Inuit people live in the north-west of America. They believe that the world was created by a mighty raven. His name was Tul-ug-auk-uk.

The beginning of Earth

In the beginning there was only a tiny raven, floating alone in the dark. There was no Earth yet – no water, no forest, no sky. There was no sound. Raven flapped his little wings. They made a noise. Raven liked that. He flapped them some more. With each flap his wings grew bigger and bigger.

Soon Raven was a giant. He flew about, exploring the emptiness around him. His mighty wings churned the darkness, making it solid, turning it to earth. Raven cawed with delight. Every time he lifted his wings he created a mountain, every time he

lowered them, he made a valley. Raven swooped down and pecked at the ground with his beak. Icy water flowed out of the rocks.

Raven could hear the water gushing and gurgling in the dark. 'I have made rivers,' he thought, 'I have made springs and lakes and the sea.'

He beat his wings on the soil and trees sprang up, filling the air with their scent. At last Raven settled on top of a mountain. His new world was full of exciting sounds and smells but he couldn't see it.

'If only I had something to see by,' Raven thought. He peered through the darkness, inspecting every corner of the Earth. At last he saw a pinprick of light, shining far down below. Raven flew towards it. The light was coming from inside a clod of earth lying on the banks of a river. He pecked at it with his beak. Suddenly the clod of earth broke in half. A golden pebble popped out. It was smooth and round and shone with a fierce, blinding light.

Raven picked up the pebble in his beak and took it high up to his mountain perch. All around him the darkness had disappeared. The sky had turned blue, the Earth was green. The waters sparkled.

'I shall call this pebble Sun,' said Raven. He hung it up in the sky, so it would shine into every corner of the Earth. Raven sighed contentedly. Now he could see the wonderful world he had created.

Coyote

There are many stories about Coyote. In some he is a trickster, in others he is a hero who helped to create the world. This story is told by the Crow people of the Great Plains.

The creation of people

In the beginning Coyote helped the Great Spirit Chief to make the world ready for people. He built the mountains, planted the forests and spread the lakes so they would shimmer in the sun. He made everything move too. Coyote pushed the waterfalls over the cliffs and made the snow swirl. He howled at the sky until the stars began to move across the heavens. Then he set about planning how to make the New People.

'Don't forget to give them a loud voice like mine,' suggested Wolf. 'Then they can howl and frighten people.'

9

'You don't want to give them a loud voice,' argued Mouse. 'They'd be much better off with a squeak like mine. That way they can talk to each other privately.'

'Never mind the voice,' cut in Bear, 'just make sure that they can stand on two feet like me. That'll leave their hands free for crushing things.'

'What a silly thing to suggest,' said Beaver. 'What they will really need is a big, flat tail like mine.'

'Ah,' replied Coyote, 'then they'll be able to build dams, just like you.'

Owl said the New People should have sharp eyes. Falcon was certain they should have a beak. Sheep suggested wool.

'Why don't we have a competition?' suggested Coyote. 'Let's all make models of the New People and I will make the best ones come alive.'

The animals fetched mud from the river and started working right away. Mouse made two mousy figures that looked exactly like him. Bear made huge bear-like shapes that could stand on two feet. Owl gave his models large eyes and a hooked beak.

Coyote worked slowly, using all the good ideas the other animals had given him. He gave his models sharp eyes like Owl's. He made them stand on two feet like Bear. Best of all he gave them his own cunning.

13

At night, while the other animals were asleep, Coyote went around looking at the different models. His were definitely the best. So he poured water over the other models until they were washed away. Then Coyote knelt under the stars and breathed life into his models, Man and Woman.

In the morning, when the animals awoke, they found the New People standing by the river. They were looking at the world with thoughtful eyes.

Thunder

For many Native American people, such as the Blackfoot of the Great Plains, Thunder is the Spirit of the storm. He is both good and bad. He makes the rain that waters the crops but he also destroys trees, animals and people.

Thunderbird

Thunderbird lived in a lodge on top of a high mountain. No one could see him, for he flew wrapped in a thick cloak of rain clouds. People could hear his wings beating behind the clouds. They could see the lightning that forked from his eyes. Wherever he went, rain fell to the ground.

Everyone was scared of Thunderbird but they were also glad when he brought the first rains. It meant the new crops would grow. Thunderbird knew the people couldn't

15

survive without him. So he demanded a heavy price for the rains: a young woman he could take back to his lodge.

The people were angry when they heard the news. But there wasn't much they could do. Without Thunderbird there would be no rain and no crops. They would all starve to death. So every year they chose a young woman to be sacrificed to the cruel Spirit.

One year the people decided not to give Thunderbird his usual sacrifice. Thunderbird was furious. All day long he flew above the village. His enormous wings sent thunder crashing through the clouds. Lightning struck one hut after another.

Then, quite suddenly, the sky cleared. Thunderbird disappeared. 'He's gone,' said a hunter, creeping out of his hut with his wife. More people came out of their homes. 'It's true,' they gasped. 'Thunderbird has gone.'

But suddenly the Spirit was back. He came swooping out from behind a mountain. With a terrible shriek he hurled a bolt of lightning at the hunter and his wife.

16

The man was knocked unconscious. Thunderbird roared. He snatched the screaming woman in his beak and, quick as a flash, was gone.

When the hunter came to, the chief told him what had happened. 'I shall get my wife back,' said the hunter.

'We can't defy Thunderbird a second time,' warned his friends. 'Besides, no one knows where his lodge is.'

'I shall find it,' said the hunter stubbornly. He filled his quiver with arrows and set off.

Thunderbird lived somewhere in the clouds, he was sure of that. He would climb the highest mountain until he found him. The hunter's journey took many days. On the way he met Bear, Beaver, Owl and Old Coyote. None of them knew where Thunderbird lived. Spring gave way to summer. The leaves turned from green to brown and then fell off the trees. But still the hunter wandered around the mountain, looking for his wife.

One day he met Raven standing outside his lodge. 'What brings you so high up the mountain?' asked the powerful bird.

'Thunderbird stole my wife,' replied the hunter. 'I am looking for his lodge.'

Raven offered him food and water.

17

'I know where Thunder-bird lives,' he said.

'Will you show me the way?' asked the hunter. Raven nodded. 'It is right above us, on the next summit. You can't see it from here because it is covered in clouds.'

'Then I must go right away,' said the hunter.

'If you go unarmed,' warned Raven, 'Thunderbird will kill you.'

'I have arrows,' said the hunter.

'They are not enough,' warned Raven, taking a feather from his wing. 'There is only one creature Thunderbird cannot harm. Me.'

He gave the hunter the feather from his wing and a magic black arrow.

'When Thunderbird threatens to kill you,' he said, 'point the feather at him. He will be forced to let you go.

'Before you do that, shoot the magic arrow through the wall of his lodge. It is made of black elk-horn. Your wife will come back with you.'

'Thank you,' said the hunter. He put the feather in his pocket and the magic arrow in his quiver. Then he hurried up the mountain.

Soon he passed through the clouds and found Thunderbird's lodge. 'Who goes there?' roared Thunderbird.

'It is I,' said the hunter. 'I have come to take my wife back home with me.'

Thunderbird roared with laughter. 'Fool,' he said. 'No one who comes here ever leaves again.'

The hunter stood his ground. Thunderbird glared. He moved forward, ready to strike. The hunter pointed Raven's feather at him.

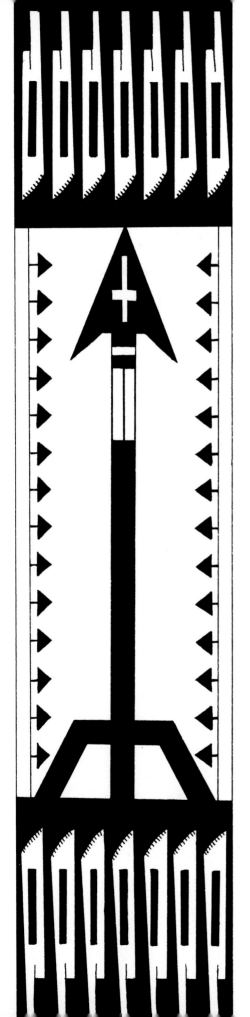

'Agh,' screamed Thunderbird. He fell back, howling with rage. The hunter fitted the magic arrow in his bow. *Tang.* The arrow went straight through the wall of the lodge, leaving a gaping hole. Bright sunlight flooded in, filling the place with light.

'I am defeated,' said Thunderbird. 'Your magic is stronger than mine. Take your wife back, but do not forget that I bring the warm rains and the crops. Your people must pray to me. They must thank me for the good I do. Then I will not need to take your women.'

'How will you hear their prayers?' asked the hunter. Thunderbird handed him a pipe. 'They must smoke their prayers to me so that I can see them.' The hunter put the pipe in his quiver. Thunderbird showed him down the mountain path through the clouds. There he found his wife waiting for him.

The couple returned to their people. They showed them the sacred pipe and told them what Thunderbird had said. From that day onwards they never saw the great Spirit again. Their descendants still hear his wings beating above the clouds to this very day but they are not afraid. They know Thunderbird will keep the promise he made to their ancestors.

Why wolves chase deer

This story is told by the Tsimshian people of British Columbia, Canada.

A long time ago the wolves gathered in a clearing by the river. They were there for The Great Howling, a festival of songs and stories. One by one the wolves stood on their hind legs and told long, exciting tales.

At night they joined together in song. They sang about hunting and feasting, about crossing great rivers and keeping warm in the cold winter. Their howling echoed all around the forest, terrifying the other animals.

Only the moon liked the wolves' howling. She hung around the tops of the pine trees, listening to their every word.

Now across the river some deer had met to tell their own stories. They heard the howling and wondered what it was. So they all trooped down to the river bank to see.

'What strange creatures,' said a doe. The deer listened to the wolves' songs. And, quite frankly, they did not believe a word they were hearing. They all started laughing. The wolves were very annoyed.

'Let's go get them,' said some of the young cubs.

'Don't be silly,' said their parents. 'Don't you see that they are much bigger and stronger than us?'

The cubs glared at the deer. The deer did look big and strong but they had one big flaw. 'Those creatures have no fangs,' cried a cub.

'You're right,' said one of the elders. 'Those beasts cannot fight back. They will make perfect prey.'

The hungry wolves leapt into the river. The deer stopped laughing right away. Too late, they'd noticed the wolves' sharp teeth. So they fled and hid in the forest.

That night they managed to escape. But ever since then, wolves have always chased deer – for they know the poor creatures have no fangs to defend themselves with.

Winter and spring

The following story is told by the Iroquois people of the eastern woodlands of the USA.

Old Man Winter ruled over the world. He had a lodge made of ice, which stood at the foot of a high mountain. From there he sent his servant North Wind to bind the world in freezing snow.

No one ever came to see the old man. People were too scared of him. Even the fire that cooked his fish dared not glow too brightly.

Once in a while, North Wind used to drop by on his way to fetch more snow from the mountain. He would share a pipe with Old Man Winter and boast about his travels around the world. North Wind loved his job.

One day, as the cold pair sat dozing on the icy floor, North Wind said: 'I think the icicles in here are melting.'

'Nonsense,' said Old Man Winter.

'The frost seems less thick too,' North Wind complained.

'It can't be,' replied the old man. But he held his hand to the fire and the frost under his fingernails started to melt.

'I tell you there's warmth in this house,' cried North Wind in a panic. He leapt to his feet and dashed out.

Old Man Winter looked around him in alarm. It was true. The fire seemed to be burning brighter. His beard felt damp with thawing frost. Suddenly there was a knock at the door.

'Who's there?' asked Old Man Winter.

'I am a friend,' replied a voice. 'Please let me in.'

'Go away,' said Old Man Winter. 'I have no friends. Only North Wind is welcome here.'

But the door opened by itself. A young man stood in the doorway, smiling.

'Greetings,' he said, and the fire leapt up to welcome him.

'How dare you come into my house?' shouted the old man. 'Don't you know who I am?'

The young man smiled. He sat by the fire and offered to fill the old man's pipe.

27

Old Man Winter could see a flicker of spring stars in his eyes. He felt a powerful warmth glowing in his coppery skin.

'I shall freeze you to death with my breath,' he threatened. 'For I am the great Winter himself, the most powerful being on Earth. The sun flees from my scowl and the world hides from my anger. When I stamp my feet, people like you get buried under falling snow.'

The young man sighed and handed Old Man Winter his pipe.

'I am not scared of you,' he said. 'You are old and weak. I am young and strong.'

'I am still strong,' insisted Old Man Winter. But he could feel his strength slipping away from him by the second.

'Don't you understand?' said the young man. 'I am Go-Hay; I am Spring. When I smile, your ice turns to water. Everywhere I walk, the soil grows warm under my feet. The trees burst into life and flowers grow in the fields. I sing and the birds wake from their sleep. Animals come out of their wintry burrows. Listen, can you not hear the blue-bird singing already?'

'Perhaps I can,' said Old Man Winter weakly.

'You were a powerful ruler,' said Go-Hay softly. 'But your time here has passed. Your lodge is melting. You must make way for me. Go now before the warm sun melts away your snowy path.'

Old Man Winter nodded feebly. Suddenly he felt weak and powerless. He trudged out of his lodge and looked around him. His snow was melting fast.

30

Green shoots were poking out of the ground. Water bubbled in a brook nearby and birds sang in the trees.

Old Man Winter hurried along the fading path up the mountain. Behind him, his lodge melted away and young saplings grew in its place. At the summit he stopped for one last moment. Even up here, there was only a small patch of snow left to show he had ever been on Earth. He touched it, and then he passed into his lodge in the sky.

At the foot of the mountain, Go-Hay started building his lodge. The sun came out from behind the clouds to greet him.

At last the long winter was over. Spring was in the air.

Bluebird and Coyote

A story from the Pima of the south-west.

Bluebird was not always blue. A long time ago he was a dull grey. He was Greybird.

One day Greybird discovered a bright blue lake. 'Perhaps if I swim in it, I shall turn blue too,' he thought. He dipped his head in the water, then studied his reflection. It was no good. He was still grey.

'You're not doing it right,' said Butterfly, who was resting on a rock nearby.

'Did you get your lovely blue colour from the lake?' asked Greybird.

'I did indeed,' said Butterfly. 'And this is what you have to do if you want to be blue like me. Bathe in the lake four times every morning for four mornings. Each time you must face a different direction: north, south, east or west. And each time you must sing to the lake, asking it for a little of its beauty.

32

If the magic works, you must sing another song, thanking it for its help. Do this before you touch anything, otherwise your new colour will disappear.'

Greybird did as Butterfly told him and on the fourth day his feathers changed into a dazzling blue. He was so happy he burst into a thankful song right away.

'I am Bluebird now,' he said, and he flew into the forest to show off his new colour.

A few days later Bluebird met Coyote. Coyote was a dull grey, just like Bluebird had been before his dip in the magic lake.

'How can I become blue like you?' asked Coyote.

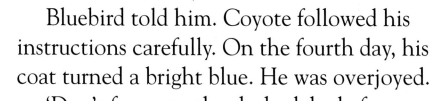

Bluebird told him. Coyote followed his instructions carefully. On the fourth day, his coat turned a bright blue. He was overjoyed.

'Don't forget to thank the lake before you touch anything,' called out Bluebird.

But Coyote was far too excited to hear him. He rushed into the forest shouting, 'Look at me – I'm blue!' Coyote was so excited he didn't look where he was going. He ran right into a tree. Coyote fell to the ground, howling in pain. When he stood up again he was covered in grey dust. He tried to brush it away but it was no use. The dust was stuck to his fur. Coyote remembered he had not sung his thank-you song to the lake. He'd lost the magic. That's why he is grey to this very day.

The first love music

The Lakota Sioux believed that flute music could make people fall in love.

The young hunter was in love. He wanted to marry the chief's daughter. But the chief's daughter didn't want to marry anyone. She preferred to stay at home with her family, laughing and telling stories round the fire. So the hunter decided to cast a spell on her.

He set out to catch an elk. He'd heard that elks were special. They could make anyone fall in love with you. All day long, the hunter trudged across the plain. It was the end of spring and most of the herds had moved to the mountain pastures.

When he reached the edge of the forest, he knelt in the bushes to study the ground. Yes, there was the trail of an elk, leading straight into the forest. He followed it, creeping painfully on his hands and knees.

35

At last the hunter saw the elk. It was in a clearing, feeding on birch leaves.

The young hunter hid behind a bush. Carefully, he put an arrow to the bow and took aim. Just then, the wind turned.

The elk turned its head sharply, sniffing the air. Then it leapt into the undergrowth. The young hunter gave chase but the elk was too fast for him. Before long it had disappeared. The hunter slowed down. He realized he was lost.

He tried to find his way back to the edge of the forest but it was no use. He seemed to be going round in circles. To make matters worse, it was getting dark.

The hunter decided to spend the night in the forest. In the morning he would make his way back to the plains. It would be easy to find a path in the morning light. He found a dry spot under a tree and settled down for the night.

He tried to sleep but he couldn't. The forest was full of noise. Animals cawed and screeched. Big cats howled. The wind blew through the branches of the trees, making them whine.

Then he heard a strange, haunting sound that he did not recognize. It rose and fell with the breeze, like the cry of a lonely ghost. Somehow it made him think of the chief's daughter. He wondered what she was doing back in the village across the plain. He fell asleep thinking of her. Towards morning he dreamt he saw a red-headed woodpecker in a tree. He was singing along to the eerie sound the hunter had heard.

'I am the spirit Wagnuka,' he sang. 'Follow me and I shall lead you to the song.'

When the hunter woke up, the woodpecker was sitting in the branches overhead.

He chirped at him and then flew off to another tree.

The hunter remembered the words of the song. 'Follow me, and I shall lead you to the song.' So he followed the bird.

Further and further into the forest Wagnuka flew. At last he settled in the branches of a cedar tree. Now the hunter could hear the weird sound from his dream again. But this time it wasn't the woodpecker singing. The sound was coming from the branches of the cedar itself.

Wagnuka pecked a hole in a small branch with his sharp beak. The wind blew through it and there it was again – the strange, haunting sound that made the hunter think of the chief's daughter. He was overjoyed. Here was a piece of magic he could take back to the village. His people would have a new kind of music to dance to. The chief's daughter would be most impressed.

The hunter cut the small branch off the tree. He stuck it under his arm and hurried back to the village.

'Have you brought meat?' asked his people. 'Have you brought elk-magic?'

'No,' he said, 'but I have brought a new kind of music.' He held up the cedar branch for everyone to see. The hunter waved the

branch around in the air. He held it up high so the wind would blow through it. It was no use. No haunting sound came out of it.

The hunter was upset. 'There must be something wrong with me,' he said. 'I have killed the magic.'

He went into the sweat-lodge to purify himself. He fasted. Then he went out of the village and prayed for a vision.

'Wagnuka,' he cried. 'Show me how to make music.'

His prayers were answered. That night he had a dream. In it Wagnuka was a red-haired man. He had a cedar branch in his hand. 'Watch carefully,' he said, 'and I will show you how to make love music.'

In the morning the young hunter cut a thin cedar branch. He hollowed it out, carved a woodpecker's head at one end and dyed it red. Then he drilled a line of holes along the top. The young hunter purified the branch by holding it in the smoke of a sage and cedar fire. At last he was ready to try out the instrument.

He stood under the cedar tree and carefully lifted the branch to his lips. As Wagnuka had shown him, he placed his fingers on the holes. Then he blew gently through the mouthpiece.

The magic worked. The strange, haunting sound filled the air, trembling and wavering. The people in the village were spellbound. They dropped their tools and hurried to the cedar tree.

'Look,' the young hunter said. 'I have made the first flute.'

Everyone in the village was impressed. Everyone said what joy the flute had brought to the village. Only the chief's daughter ignored the haunting music.

'How can I cast a spell on her?' wondered the hunter desperately. 'How can I make her fall in love with me?'

He thought about the problem for a long time. Then he had an idea. He would capture all the beautiful sounds of the world

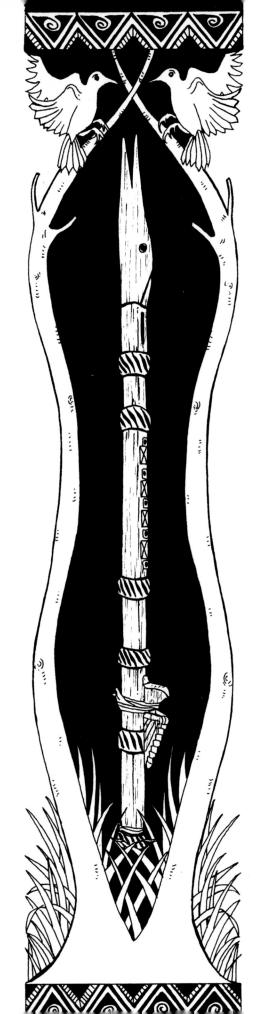

in his flute and make a love song. She would not be able to resist that.

For many days the hunter listened to the world around him. He learnt the sound of the birds and the waterfalls, he memorized the whispering of the grass and the sighing of the evening breeze. Then he composed a special song, full of the joy and hope and sadness of life.

At night he stood outside the girl's *tipi*. He put the flute to his lips and started playing. The girl tried to ignore the music but she couldn't help listening. As if in a dream, she stood up and left the *tipi*.

She only intended to stand outside so she could hear the music better but her feet led her towards the hunter. She tried to resist but the music was too powerful. It drew her closer and closer. Soon she was standing right next to the man who loved her.

'I love you,' she said. 'I love you so much.'

'I love you too,' said the hunter.

Next morning all the braves in the village heard how the chief's daughter had fallen in love with the young hunter. They too made flutes and learnt how to play them. In no time at all the flute was being played in every village on the plains, filling the world with its music of love.

42

Death and Heaven

The Skidi Pawnees in Nebraska believe that the Milky Way is a long white road across the heavens. The souls of the dead travel along it to get to the Last Hunting Ground.

The last journey

Wahu was sad and lonely. All his life he'd been a good hunter. He'd provided for his family. Now his wife was dead. His children were married. There was nothing to do but walk the dog and think of the past.

Wahu sat on the river's edge. He felt tired. His bones ached. Strange voices whispered in his head. 'Come to us, Wahu,' they chanted. 'We are your dear departed friends. We miss you.'

Wahu thought how wonderful his life had been when he was still surrounded by his loved ones. He remembered the hunting and

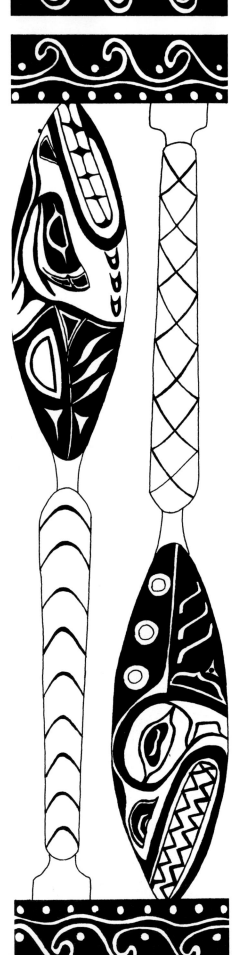

the fishing. He thought of the stories he had told with his friends around the fire. Perhaps they could do all that again in the Last Hunting Ground, up there in the sky.

Wahu got into his canoe. He picked up his paddle and started rowing. His dog barked from the riverbank. 'Go back, little friend,' he called. 'This is a journey I must make alone.'

The dog whined, and went back to their empty hut. Wahu smiled sadly. He would not see his faithful companion again. He was alone now, on the last journey to the sky.

He paddled deeper and deeper into the forest. His arms ached but he did not stop paddling until he had reached two enormous rocks on either side of the river. Beyond them he could see White Water. It was the gate that led to the Last Hunting Ground. Two shadowy figures appeared on the bank. One of them beckoned, and Wahu stopped the canoe.

'You have reached the sacred gate,' said one. 'Do you come alone?'

'Yes,' said Wahu sadly. 'I come alone.'

The other figure pointed to the shallows. 'No,' he said. 'You have brought a trusted friend with you.'

Wahu heard a familiar bark behind him.

44

He turned. His dog had followed him there.

'Welcome back,' he said happily.

The two figures gave the canoe a push towards the rapids. Wahu hugged his dog. Then he threw away the paddle. They had no use for it now. The White Water would carry them over the edge of the rocks towards the Last Hunting Ground.

Notes

Blackfoot (pp4, 15)
The Blackfoot people got their name from the black-dyed moccasins (soft shoes) they wore.

Crow (pp4, 9)
A people of the northern plains. They call themselves the Bird People.

Elk (pp35, 37)
Elk are a kind of deer. They are shy, and can run very fast. They move up the mountains in the summer to feed and come down to the plains in winter.

Great Plains (pp9, 15)
The rolling prairies and grasslands that lie between the Mississippi Valley and the Rocky Mountains.

Inuit (say In-you-it) (pp4, 6)
The name for the Native American peoples of the far north, from Alaska to Greenland.

Iroquois (say Ear-oh-kwah) (pp4, 26)
A people who used to live in the eastern woodlands of the USA. The area is now New York State.

Medicine man (p5)
A person with powers of healing. He used medicines that had been given strength or made sacred.

Music (pp35, 40–42)
Music is important to Native American peoples. They have drums, rattles and flutes.
Flutes were sometimes used for special dances and for playing love music.

Pawnee (pp4, 43)
Farmers and buffalo hunters who lived on the plains. The name Pawnee means 'horn'. The men would shave the sides of their heads and grease up the hair on top to look like a horn.

NATIVE NORTH AMERICA

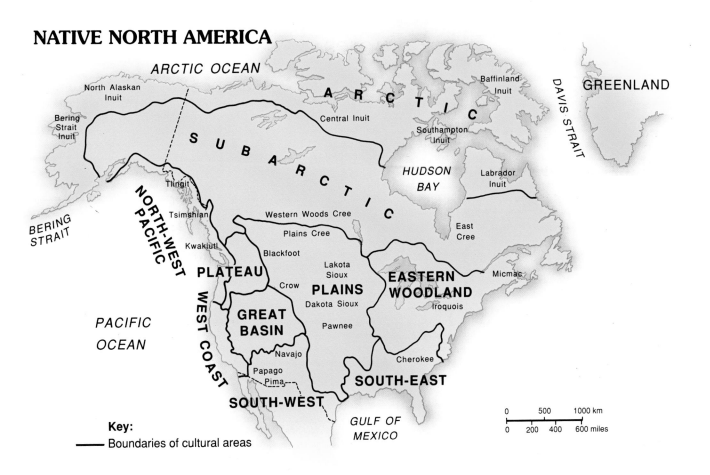

Pima (say Pee-ma) (pp4, 32)
The Pima lived in what is now Arizona. They were farmers who grew corn, cotton, tobacco and other crops.

Raven (pp6–8, 17, 20)
Raven is both a creator and a trickster. The Native Americans of the north-west thought of Raven as the maker of the world and the bringer of light.

Sioux (say Su) (pp4, 35)
The Sioux lived on the Great Plains. They lived in *tipis*, hunted buffalo and rode horses.

Sweat-lodge (pp40)
A shelter where stones are heated on a fire and water is poured over them. The steam rising from the stones cleanses the person having a 'sweat'. People went to the sweat-lodge before important events.

47

Thunderbird (pp15–22)
Thunderbird is an enormous bird who beats his wings to make thunder. He brings the spring storms that help the crops to grow.

Tipi (**say tee-pee**) (pp4, 42, 47)
Cone-shaped tents. Many people in the Great Plains lived in *tipis*. *Tipis* had frames of poles with buffalo hide stretched over them. They were often beautifully painted.

Tsimshian (say Shim-she-un) (pp4, 23)
The Tsimshian came from the north-west Pacific coast. They mainly ate salmon from the sea. There were many ceremonies to thank the ocean for providing fish.

Wigwam (say wig-wom) (p4)
The peoples of the east built wigwams. They were like *tipis* but usually smaller. The poles were covered with rush mats and bark.

Further reading

Grandfather Speak: Native American Folk-Tales of Lenape People (Interlink, 1995)
Indian Heroes and Great Chieftains by Charles A. Eastman (Bison Books, 1991)
Native Americans by James Wilson (Wayland, 1992)

Pale Moon: Myths and Legends of Native Americans (ICS Books, 1995)
Storytelling Stone: Traditional Native American Myths and Tales (Yearling, 1996)
Wolf Tales: Native American Children's Stories (Ancient City, 1997)